Fish

Fish

Published by
Heron Books, Inc.
20950 SW Rock Creek Road
Sheridan, OR 97378

heronbooks.com

Special thanks to all the teachers and students who
provided feedback instrumental to this edition.

Third Edition © 1978, 2022 Heron Books.
All Rights Reserved

ISBN: 978-0-89-739281-5

Any unauthorized copying, translation, duplication or distribution, in whole
or in part, by any means, including electronic copying, storage or transmission,
is a violation of applicable laws.

The Heron Books name and the heron bird symbol are registered trademarks
of Delphi Schools, Inc.

Printed in the USA

30 October 2022

At Heron Books, we think learning should be engaging and fun. It should be hands-on and allow students to move at their own pace.

To facilitate this we have created a learning guide that will help any student progress through this book, chapter by chapter, with confidence and interest.

Get learning guides at
heronbooks.com/learningguides.

For teacher resources,
such as a final exam, email
teacherresources@heronbooks.com.

We would love to hear from you!
Email us at *feedback@heronbooks.com*.

IN THIS BOOK

Chapter 1
HOW ARE FISH ALIKE?......................................3
    Fish Live in Water 3
    Fish Have Fins 4
    Fish Have Gills.......................................4
    Most Fish Have Scales 5
    Fish Are Cold-Blooded............................6
    How Are Fish Alike?................................6
        Let's Do This: How Fish Are Alike 7

Chapter 2
THE LIFE OF A FISH..11
    Egg 11
    Baby Fish 13
    Adult 14
    Laying Eggs 14

Chapter 3
SO MANY FISH!...17
    Tuna...17
    Herrings, Sardines and Anchovies 19
    Salmon...20
    Trout 21

Catfish	23
Eels	24
Sharks	26
Skates and Rays	28
Sea Horses	29
So Many Fish!	30
Let's Do This: Find Out More	31

Chapter 4
LIVING WITH FISH 35

Food	35
Fishing for Food	37
Fishing for Sport	39
Let's Do This: More Activities with Fish	42
Take Care of Some Pet Fish	42
Feed Some Wild Fish	43
Study Fish in a Pet Store	44
Study Fish at a Fish Market	45
Study Fish at a Fish Farm or Hatchery	46
Study Fish at an Aquarium	47
Study Fish at a Museum	48
Study Wild Fish Underwater	49
Go on a Fishing Trip	50
Watch a Video About Fish	51
Do Your Own Special Fish Project	52

Chapter 1

How Are Fish Alike?

Chapter 1

How Are Fish Alike?

Fish are very special animals. Of all the animals that live in the water, fish are the best swimmers. Many of the ways that fish are alike have something to do with why they are such good swimmers.

Here are some important ways fish are alike.

FISH LIVE IN WATER

Their bodies are shaped so they can move through the water easily.

Most fish can live for only a few minutes out of water.

HOW ARE FISH ALIKE?

FISH HAVE FINS

Fins are what fish use to push their bodies through the water or to steer with.

FISH HAVE GILLS

Gills are part of a fish's body right behind its head. Gills look like slits from the outside.

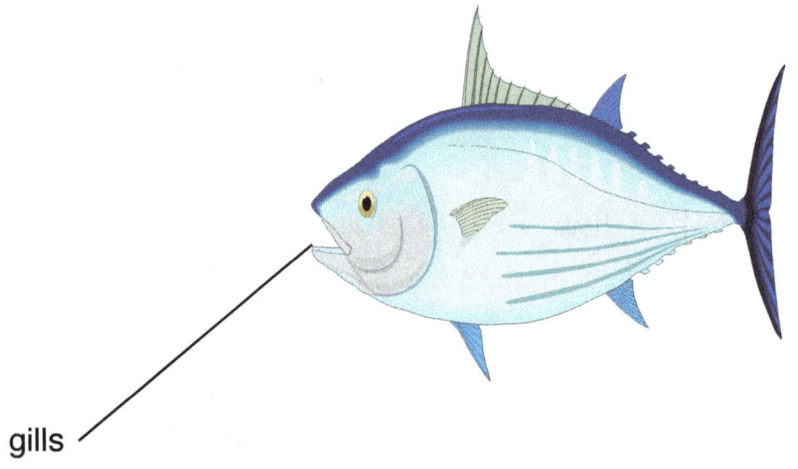

Gills have the same purpose as lungs do for people. Fish use their gills to breathe tiny parts of air that are in the water. They take in water through their mouths and let it out through their gill slits. When the water goes by their gills, the air that is in it gets picked up by the gills and taken into the fish's blood.

When a fish swims faster, more water goes into its mouth and out through its gills, so it gets more air when it is working harder.

MOST FISH HAVE SCALES

Scales are little sheets of thin stiff material.

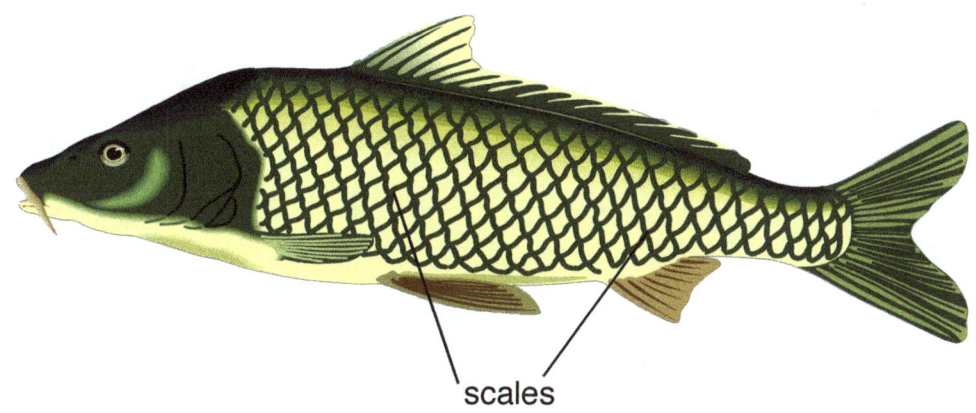
scales

Scales cover and protect a fish's body. Each row of scales partly covers the one next to it, from back to front, kind of like shingles on the roof of a house.

If you feel a fish's scales, you will notice that they feel smooth if you rub from front to back. They feel rough if you rub from back to front. Scales help the fish move smoothly forward through the water.

FISH ARE COLD-BLOODED

Animals that are **cold-blooded** have bodies that change when the temperature around them changes. The blood and body temperature of fish changes as the water temperature they swim in changes.

HOW ARE FISH ALIKE?

They live in water.

They have fins.

They have gills.

Most have scales.

They are cold-blooded.

LET'S DO THIS!
How Fish Are Alike

For this activity you will need

- access to the internet, picture books or magazines of fish
- drawing materials
- Optional: a real fish in a tank will work for some steps

Steps

FISH LIVE IN WATER

1. Look at an online video of fish living in water. Notice how their bodies are shaped.

FISH HAVE FINS

2. Look at pictures of lots of different fish and notice their fins.

3. Look at an online video of fish swimming. Notice how they use their fins to move.

FISH HAVE GILLS

4. Look at pictures of lots of different fish and notice their gills.

5. If you can, find an online video of a live fish swimming that shows the gills working close up.

MOST FISH HAVE SCALES

6. Look at pictures of different fish scales.

HOW ARE FISH ALIKE?

FISH ARE COLD-BLOODED

7. Explain to another person what it means to say fish are cold-blooded.

COMPARE A FISH TO ANOTHER WATER ANIMAL

8. Choose a water animal that is not a fish, such as a whale, dolphin, sea turtle, frog.

9. Look at pictures of fish and of your water animal. Notice what is the same and what is different about the two.

10. Tell another person what you found out that was the same and what was different.

PUT IT TOGETHER

11. Draw a picture of a fish swimming in water, including a thermometer to show the temperature of the water and the temperature of the fish. Show the fins, gills and the scales. Label the drawing with the five ways fish are alike.

12. Show your drawing to another person, and explain the five ways fish are alike.

Chapter 2

The Life of a Fish

Chapter 2

The Life of a Fish

EGG

The life of a fish starts in an egg. Mother fish lay their eggs in the weeds and on rocks under water. They lay many, many eggs. Some fish lay over a thousand eggs at one time!

eggs

With some kinds of fish, the father or mother fish guards the eggs from other fish. In one kind of fish, the eggs are kept safe in the *mouth* of the father fish!

THE LIFE OF A FISH

But with most kinds of fish, the mother and father fish either just leave the eggs or they hide the eggs and then leave them.

Often many of the eggs get eaten by other fish. But there are usually some eggs left to hatch.

BABY FISH

After several days the baby fish hatch out of the eggs. They can swim and eat as soon as they are born.

Many of the baby fish also get eaten by bigger fish.

Now you can see why there are so many eggs! With so many of the eggs and baby fish getting eaten, there *have* to be a lot of them so that some of them can live long enough to grow up.

Some of the baby fish usually are good enough at hiding or running away that they grow up to be big fish.

THE LIFE OF A FISH

ADULT

Fish spend their lives swimming around looking for things to eat (and staying away from things that might eat them), so they can grow bigger and bigger.

LAYING EGGS

Then someday they lay eggs of their own, so there can be more baby fish again.

Chapter 3

So Many Fish!

Chapter 3

So Many Fish!

All fish are alike in certain ways, but there are so many different kinds of fish!

Some fish are short and fat and lumpy, and look like rocks or clumps of seaweed. These kinds of fish usually spend most of their time on the bottom, and swim slowly, mainly by moving their fins.

Other fish are long and sleek, and live mainly near the top of the water where they can swim far and fast. These kinds of fish usually can swim very fast by moving their whole tail, using their fins mostly to steer.

Here are some of the most familiar kinds of fish found in the waters in or near North America.

TUNA

Tuna are large fish that live near the top of the water in the open ocean. They are good swimmers and sometimes jump and splash on the surface.

Small tuna swim together in groups called **schools**. Bigger tuna more often swim alone. Some kinds of tuna get quite big and may weigh as much as a man!

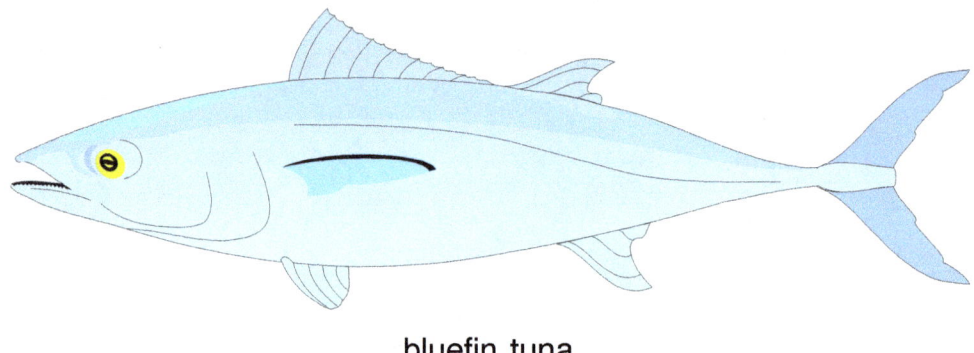

bluefin tuna

Tuna are mostly blue and silver colored. They eat smaller fish.

skipjack tuna

Tuna are important to people because they are used as food. Fishers (people who catch fish) go out to sea in boats and catch tuna in big nets.

HERRINGS, SARDINES AND ANCHOVIES

Herrings, sardines and anchovies are small fish that live out in the ocean and swim in big schools. These are some of the smaller fish that tuna eat.

Herrings are the biggest of the three and may grow to be a foot or so long. Sardines rarely grow bigger than a half a foot long, and anchovies are usually even smaller. All these fish are mostly silver in color.

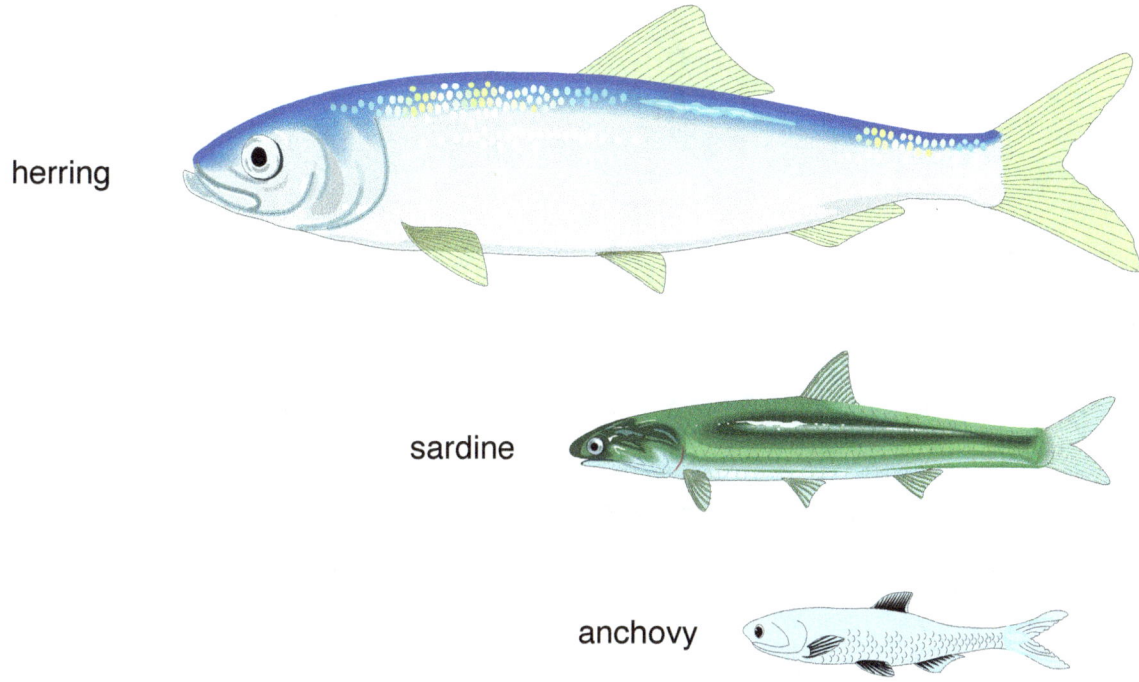

These fish all eat very tiny plants and animals that live near the top of the ocean. They all swim in large schools for protection from bigger fish that want to catch and eat them.

Sardines, herrings and anchovies are caught by fishers all over the world. They are caught from boats by using large nets. You can find cans of herrings, sardines and anchovies in almost any grocery store.

SO MANY FISH!

SALMON

Most salmon grow to be one to two feet long. Some kinds get as long as three feet.

Although salmon hatch in freshwater streams, they go to sea and live most of their lives in the ocean.

Once a year, the adult salmon swim from the ocean back to the rivers where they hatched. They swim way upstream (**upstream** means up the river away from the ocean). They even jump up waterfalls to get upstream. Salmon have an amazing ability to find their way from the ocean to the stream where they hatched.

When they get upstream, the salmon lay eggs. Many kinds of adult salmon die after that. Other kinds swim back to the ocean. The eggs hatch and the baby salmon spend part of their first year growing up in the rivers. During this time they are called **smolts**.

When the young smolts are partly grown (about ten inches long or so) they swim out to the ocean to live and grow into adult salmon. After a year or more they swim back up to where they were born in order to lay eggs.

The meat of salmon is pink, and has a good flavor. Fishers catch salmon when the fish come back from the ocean to swim up the rivers. Sometimes they use big nets that catch almost all the fish that try to swim up the river. But if all the salmon get caught, none will get up the river to lay eggs, and next time there will be no salmon coming back to that river. This is why, in most places, fishers are careful to let enough salmon go by their nets, so there will be plenty of eggs and new smolts.

TROUT

Trout are a lot like salmon, but most trout live their whole lives in freshwater rivers and lakes.

Like salmon, they may be from one to three feet long when fully grown, although they are usually not longer than two feet. Trout are usually silver colored and often have many spots on their bodies.

One kind, called rainbow trout, has pink or purple stripes.

SO MANY FISH!

rainbow trout

Trout eat smaller fish and insects that fall in the water or fly close to the surface. Some trout will eat worms too.

Many fishers like to fish for trout. They are good to eat and they are fun to catch. Fishers try to fool the trout into biting at artificial "flies" made out of colored feathers tied to a fish hook. They use a special kind of fishing rod so they can "cast" their flies a long distance. They whip the fishing line back and forth in the air until they can make the fly come down right where they think a hungry trout is. This is called fly fishing.

SO MANY FISH!

There is a kind of rainbow trout called steelhead that behaves like the salmon. It hatches and begins growing up in streams, then goes to sea, and later comes back to lay eggs in the stream. These trout grow up to three feet long.

CATFISH

Catfish live on the bottom of rivers and lakes. They get their name because they have things called barbels on their heads that look like the whiskers of a cat. Some kinds of catfish are called bullheads because they have a very broad head and a flat snout.

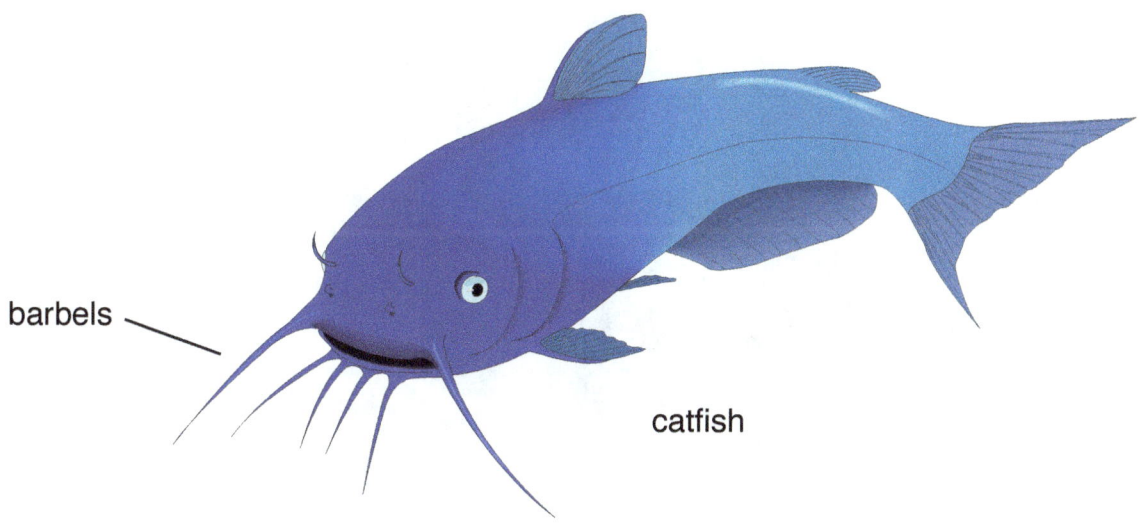

barbels

catfish

SO MANY FISH!

Catfish are one kind of fish that doesn't have scales. Instead they have bony plates for protection. Some kinds of catfish are blue, some are yellow and some are gray and tan. Some kinds usually weigh about five pounds. Others can grow to weigh as much as a hundred pounds!

Catfish eat clams and grass, and almost anything else they find on the bottom of the pond or stream that is small enough to eat.

When their ponds dry up, some catfish bury themselves in the mud and live there until rains fill the pond again.

Many people fish for catfish to eat. They are generally easy to catch. Some people raise catfish for food in little ponds.

EELS

Eels are long, skinny fish. They live in rivers and in oceans. Most eels grow to be about five feet long. Some big ocean eels called conger eels may grow to be as long as 12 feet!

conger eel

All eels found in rivers of the eastern United States are born in the ocean, in one certain area off the southeast coast of the United States called the Sargasso Sea. While they are still very little, they swim to freshwater rivers.

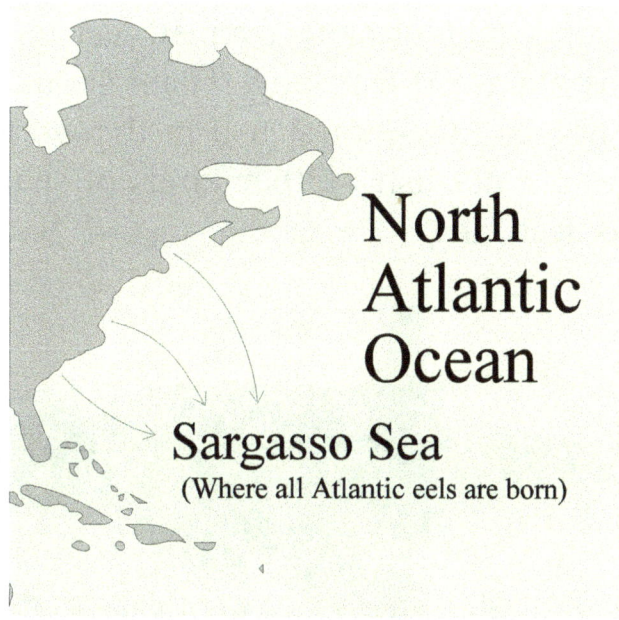

The male eels stay near the mouth of the river, but the females often swim far upstream. They stay there for several years, but when they are ready to make baby eels, they all swim back to the place in the sea where they were born. Nobody knows why Atlantic coast eels do this, just as nobody knows why salmon swim in the opposite direction to lay their eggs.

Pacific Ocean eels such as the California moray and others are only found in salt water along the coasts.

Most eels are light brown in color. Some have many colors on them. They eat almost anything. In winter, eels may bury themselves in the mud for months. Some people catch eels for food.

SO MANY FISH!

SHARKS

Sharks are large fish that live in the ocean. They are usually gray and white in color.

The great white shark may grow to over 40 feet long. The whale shark can grow as big as 60 feet long. That's about as long as 4 full-sized cars! These are the largest fish in the world. (Whales are bigger, but whales are not fish.) Other kinds of sharks may be only about three to six feet long.

whale shark

Sharks are quite different from other kinds of fish. They are another kind of fish that don't have scales. They have thick and tough skin instead. Shark skeletons are made entirely of tough **cartilage**, similar to what makes up our ears. The cartilage never hardens into bone as it does in other animals. This makes them weigh less, and lets them move quickly and easily through water. Their teeth are made of something similar to human teeth except stronger, and sharp new teeth keep growing in as the old ones fall out.

Unlike most other big fish that usually swallow the fish they eat whole, sharks can bite away pieces of fish with their sharp teeth.

Most sharks are quite shy and stay away from people, but some, like the great white shark, will sometimes attack people.

One of the shy kinds is the strange-looking hammerhead shark. Can you see how it gets its name?

The largest shark, the whale shark, is harmless. There are many different sorts of sharks with different manners.

Most fishers don't like sharks because they can damage fish nets with their teeth if they try to eat fish caught in the nets. But some fishers catch certain kinds of sharks for their meat and their skin.

SO MANY FISH!

SKATES AND RAYS

Skates and rays are related to sharks, but where sharks look a lot like most other fish, skates and rays look very different. They all have flat bodies with wide side fins that look like wings and long whip-like tails.

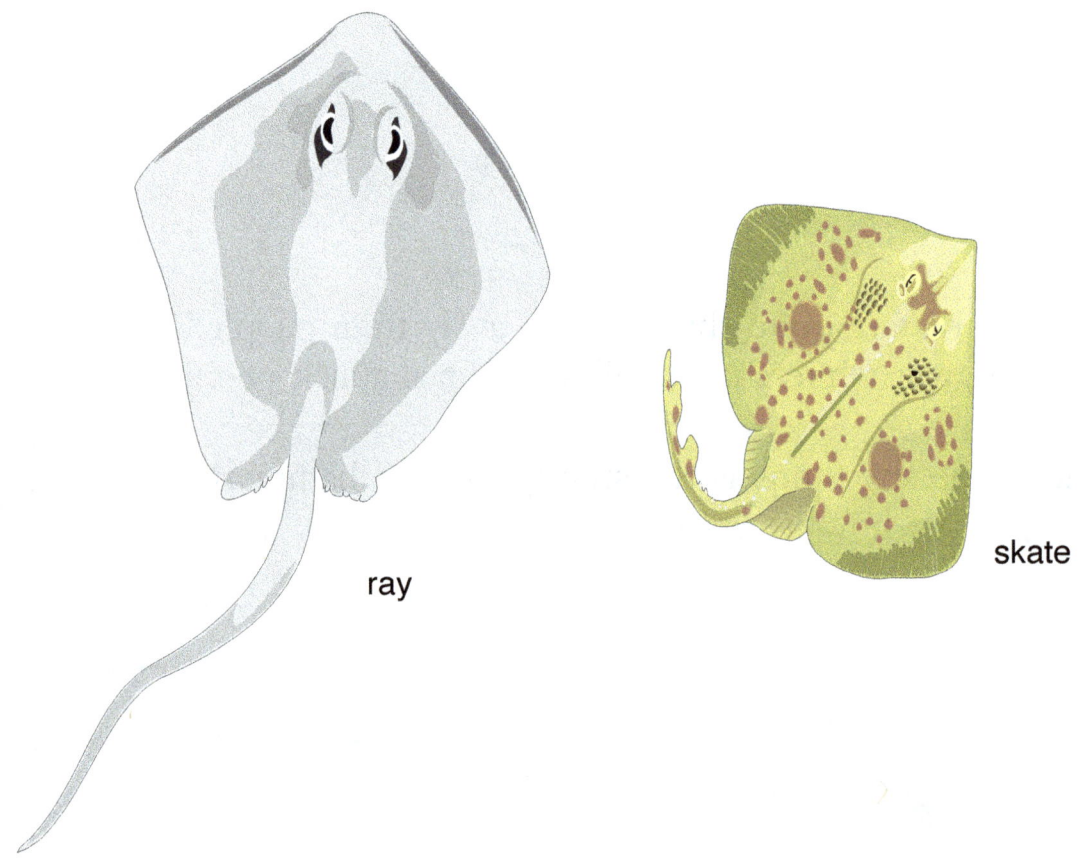

ray

skate

Skates and rays are usually dark gray or brown in color; some may have spots or other markings.

One difference between skates and rays is how they defend themselves. Most rays have a poisonous stinger in their tail. Skates don't have stingers, but they have sharp spikes along the middle of their tail and up the back.

Skates are usually smaller than rays. Most skates are less than five feet long, but some rays may be as much as ten feet long. The giant devil ray (also known as the manta ray) may be over 20 feet long!

Most skates and rays live on the ocean bottom and eat crabs and clams and other small bottom dwellers. But the giant devil ray swims in open water nearer the surface and scoops up small fish and other creatures with its huge mouth.

SEA HORSES

The sea horse is an unusual sort of fish. It is one to six inches long, and its head looks a bit like the head of a horse. Its body is covered with hard bony scales. A seahorse uses its long slender tail to hold onto seaweed, and swims by waving the fin on its back.

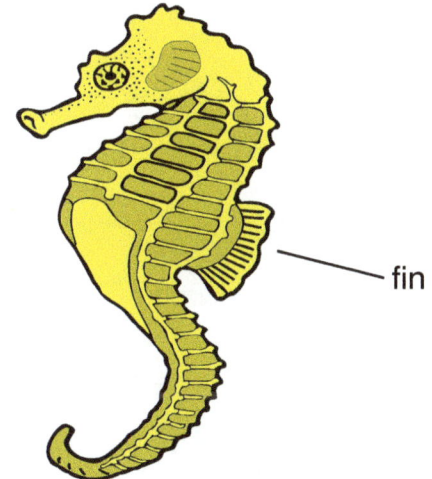

Sea horses live in warm oceans. They live around seaweeds and are colored brown and green like seaweeds. They swim very slowly and eat very, very small animals in the water.

Another way they are unusual is that after the mother sea horses lay eggs, the father sea horses keep the eggs in a pouch on their bellies until they hatch.

SO MANY FISH!

These are just a few of the many, many different kinds of fish there are in the rivers, ponds, lakes and oceans of the world.

There are fish who live so deep in the ocean that they are always in the dark. They are some of the scariest-looking fish! There are poisonous fish, and fish that look like plants. There are see-through fish and fish that look like a big blob. People are discovering new kinds of fish all the time.

LET'S DO THIS!
Find Out More

For this activity you will need

- access to internet
- drawing materials

Steps

1. Choose at least three kinds of fish you would like to learn about. You can find out more about one of the fish discussed in this book, or choose a different kind of fish. To get an idea of which fish to choose, you can search for "different kinds of fish."

2. Write down the fish you chose.

3. Have an adult help you find a short online video or article for children about the fish you chose. Find out about your fish, including their names, where they live, what they eat, and some things you thought were interesting about them. Take notes so you can use them later.

4. Draw a picture of each of your fish. Try to make your pictures show what makes each of these fish special.

5. Show your drawings to another person, and answer any questions.

Chapter 4

Living with Fish

Chapter 4

Living with Fish

Fish live in water, and people live on land, so most people do not see wild fish very often. But even so, there are many ways that fish and people affect each other.

FOOD

Fish living in ponds and streams help keep the water clean by eating weeds and insects. Fish eat baby mosquitoes that otherwise might grow up and bite other animals or people.

LIVING WITH FISH

Ocean fish help keep the ocean clean in much the same way. Small fish eat even smaller ocean plants and animals. Bigger fish eat the small fish, and even bigger fish eat them.

This is a good thing, because without big fish there could be too many little fish. Without little fish there could be too many tiny fish. And without tiny fish there could be too many other tiny animals and plants in the ponds and streams and oceans.

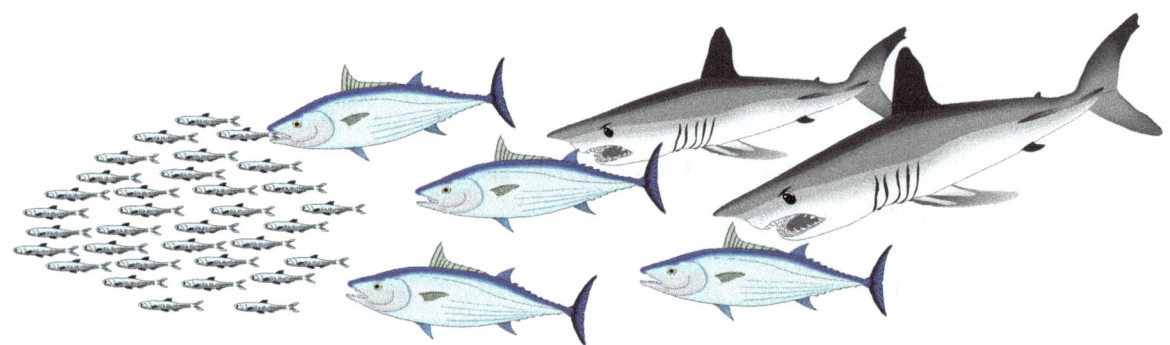

But what keeps there from being too many big fish? Well, lots of things eat big fish.

Some birds eat fish. Land animals like bears and raccoons also like to eat fish.

This chain of plants being eaten by smaller fish, smaller fish being caught and eaten by bigger fish, and the bigger fish being caught and eaten by still bigger fish or other animals is one example of a **food chain**.

It is called a chain because everything is connected, from plants to animals that eat plants, to animals that eat other animals. The food chain is nature's way of making sure all the creatures get fed. People also eat fish, so people are part of this food chain.

FISHING FOR FOOD

Most of the fish that people eat are ocean fish, like tuna and salmon and sardines. All over the world, fishers go out in the ocean on boats to catch fish.

Fishing boats come in all sizes, from small boats that carry only a few fishermen to huge "factory" ships. These big ships are almost like a floating city. Fishers can stay at sea living and working there for months at a time.

After the fish are caught, they are usually taken to a processing plant where the meat of the fish is separated from the skin and bones and other parts. The meat may be packed in cans, or delivered to markets fresh or frozen. Factory ships can do this processing right on board. That is why they are called factory ships.

The skin and bones and other parts of the fish are usually ground up and sold as fertilizer to help farmers on land grow better crops. So people get as much good as they can out of the fish that are caught.

Most fish are caught by spreading big nets to trap them. The boat spreads the net in a big circle around the place where the fish are, then slowly closes it up so the fish are caught inside. Then the net is hauled on board and the fish are dumped in the bottom of the boat.

Sometimes big fish such as sharks come to where the fishing boats are, to try to eat the fish being collected in the nets. Fishers don't like this because the big fish eat the fish the fishers are trying to catch, and sometimes they tear holes in the nets, and the fish get away.

FISHING FOR SPORT

People also catch fish for sport. Sport fishing is usually done with a fishing pole and a long thin line wound on a reel. At the end of the line is a hook to catch the fish.

Something needs to be put on the hook to get the fish to bite it. Sometimes this is food the fish like, or it could be something made to look like food, maybe a small fish or a fly. This kind of pretend food is called a **lure**.

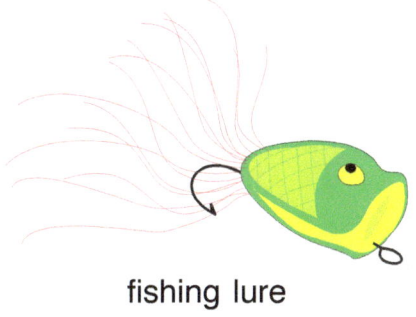

fishing lure

To make it easier to "feel" when a fish bites the lure on the other end of the line, fishers use the smallest hooks and the thinnest lines they can for the fish they want to catch. Then they have to be careful not to break the line when they are trying to pull in the fish. That is part of what makes sport fishing a challenge (and more fun).

LIVING WITH FISH

Many fishers just catch the fish and let them go. Then they have to be careful to use hooks that don't hurt the fish very much.

Sport fishing is done in both salt water and fresh water. Fish that don't give up easily but fight to get free of the hook are the favorite sport fish. The marlin is one of the favorite ocean sport fish. Bass and trout are favorite freshwater sport fish.

marlin   bass   trout

LIVING WITH FISH

Some people try to catch fish by going after them under the water, using a breathing tube called a **snorkle** or an air tank. These people use small nets or spears to catch the fish.

People also go under water just to look at the fish and find out how they live, or to take pictures of them. Usually they go looking for the most unusual or colorful fish, like tropical fish. Many of these tiny, colorful fish are caught and sold for people to keep at home in aquariums. People like them because they are unusual and pretty, and fun to watch.

People use and enjoy fish in many ways. Fish are an important part of what makes this world an interesting place to be.

LIVING WITH FISH

LET'S DO THIS!
More Activities with Fish

TAKE CARE OF SOME PET FISH

For this activity you will need

- home aquarium with fish
- drawing materials

Steps

1. Get permission to take care of the fish in the aquarium every day for a few days.

2. Find out how often the fish need to be fed and what they eat, and anything else that needs to be done to take care of them.

3. Find out what each type of fish is and where it comes from. Try to find out something you didn't already know about the fish.

4. Draw a picture of each type of fish in the aquarium.

5. Write or tell another person what you found out, and show your pictures.

FEED SOME WILD FISH

For this activity you will need

- access to a pond or river with fish
- bread you can crumble
- drawing materials

Steps

1. Go to a pond or a river with some bread you can crumble, some drawing paper and a pencil.

2. Look for a place where the water is clear and you can see a few fish swimming. If you are at a river, find a spot where the water isn't moving too fast.

3. Throw some small pieces of bread on the water, and watch to see if some fish come to eat it. You may have to wait a while for the fish to find the bread.

4. Keep feeding the fish a little bread at a time until they are not hungry any more or your bread is all gone.

5. Watch the fish closely while they are eating and draw a picture of what you can see.

6. See if the fish look like any you have learned about in this book. If so, write down your guess about what kind they are.

7. Write or tell another person what you saw, and show your picture.

LIVING WITH FISH

STUDY FISH IN A PET STORE

For this activity you will need

- access to a pet store that has a lot of fish
- drawing materials

Steps

1. Go to a pet store or an aquarium store where they have a lot of fish. Tell the person in charge of the store why you are there and ask permission to study the fish.

2. Look at all the fish and pick three kinds that are your favorites.

3. Find out what their names are, what they eat, and how to take care of them.

4. Find some different fish that eat other things.

5. Draw a picture of your three fish and write the name of it on the picture.

6. Write or tell another person what you learned, and show your pictures.

STUDY FISH AT A FISH MARKET

For this activity you will need

- access to a fish market
- notepad

Steps

1. Go to a market where they sell fish. Tell the person in charge why you are there and ask permission to look at the fish.

2. Look at all the different kinds of fish that are for sale and find out what their names are. Write down the names. Ask the person behind the counter to tell you where they were caught and how fresh they are (they may not know).

3. Go to the canned food part of the store and look for canned fish. Usually they will have tuna fish, sardines and salmon in cans, and maybe some other kinds too. If you haven't tried them before, you might want to buy some sardines or other kind of fish to take home for a meal.

4. Look up the fish you wrote the names of online to see what they looked like before they were caught.

5. Write or tell another person what you did, and what you learned.

STUDY FISH AT A FISH FARM OR HATCHERY

For this activity you will need

- access to a fish farm or hatchery
- drawing materials

Steps

1. A **fish farm** is a place where fish are raised for food. A **fish hatchery** is a place where fish are raised until they are big enough to let go in streams and rivers. Go to one of these places.

2. See if someone there will give you a tour and tell you about it. Find out what kind of fish are raised there. Find out what they are fed and how long it takes for them to grow up.

3. Look at the baby fish and the big fish, and draw pictures of them.

4. Write or tell another person what you learned, and show your pictures.

STUDY FISH AT AN AQUARIUM

For this activity you will need

- access to an aquarium
- drawing materials

Steps

1. Go to an aquarium and look at all the fish.

2. Pick at least three kinds of fish that are your favorites.

3. Draw a picture of each one, and put the name of the fish on each picture.

4. Find out where they come from and how they live, and write that down too.

5. Write or tell another person what you learned, and show your pictures.

LIVING WITH FISH

STUDY FISH AT A MUSEUM

For this activity you will need

- access to a science museum that has a fish display
- drawing materials

Steps

1. Go to a science museum and look at all the displays about fish.

2. Pick your favorite display and draw a picture of it.

3. Learn all you can about the one you picked from the display. If this was not a big display with more than one type of fish, find another one you like and draw a picture of it too.

4. Keep doing this until you have learned all about at least three types of fish.

5. Write or tell another person what you learned, and show your drawings.

STUDY WILD FISH UNDERWATER

For this activity you will need

- someone who can take you snorkeling or diving
- drawing materials

Steps

1. Go swimming underwater with a snorkel or air tank with someone who knows how.

2. If you can do this, look at all the different fish.

3. When you get back, see if you can find out the names of some of the fish you saw. Find out what you can about those fish.

4. Draw a picture that shows what it was like to look at a fish under water.

5. Write or tell another person what you learned, and show your drawing.

LIVING WITH FISH

GO ON A FISHING TRIP

For this activity you will need

- someone who can take you fishing
- fishing equipment
- drawing materials

Steps

1. Go on a fishing trip with someone who knows how to fish.

2. Learn all you can about fishing equipment and the kinds of fish he or she likes to catch.

3. Find out where these fish live and what is the best way to catch them.

4. If you catch some, look at them closely and feel their fins and their scales.

5. Draw a picture to show everything you notice about the way the fish look.

6. Write or tell another person what you learned, and show your drawing.

WATCH A VIDEO ABOUT FISH

For this activity you will need

- access to internet
- globe or map
- drawing materials

Steps

1. Have an adult help you find a short online video for children about a fish that you want to learn more about. You might get a video on fish that live in the dark, or poisonous fish. Watch the video, and notice things you have learned about fish, like what makes them fish, the different parts of their lives, and so on.

2. Look at a globe or map to find the place where the fish in the video live.

3. Decide what parts of the video you liked best, and draw pictures to show what happened in that part.

4. Write or tell another person what you have learned about fish that you noticed in the video, and show your drawings.

LIVING WITH FISH

DO YOUR OWN SPECIAL FISH PROJECT

Steps

1. Think of a project about fish that you can do that isn't on this list. For example, you could get your own aquarium, or maybe you know someone who worked on a fishing boat out at sea and you could learn about that from that person.

2. Tell another person what you want to do, and how you will do it.

3. Do your project.

4. Write or tell another person everything you did, and what you learned.

www.ingramcontent.com/pod-product-compliance
Lightning Source LLC
Chambersburg PA
CBHW081354040426

42450CB00016B/3436